New Vanguard • 119

Bronze Age War Chariots

Nic Fields · Illustrated by Brian Delf

First published in Great Britain in 2006 by Osprey Publishing,
Midland House, West Way, Botley, Oxford OX2 0PH, UK
44-02 23rd St, Suite 219, Long Island City, NY 11101, USA
Email: info@ospreypublishing.com

Osprey Publishing is part of the Osprey Group.

Transferred to digital print on demand 2011

First published 2006
4th impression 2008

Printed and bound by Cadmus Communications, USA

A CIP catalogue record for this book is available from the British Library

ISBN: 978 1 84176 944 8

Page layout by Melissa Orrom Swan, Oxford, UK
Index by Alan Thatcher
Originated by PPS Grasmere Ltd, Leeds, UK

Author's note
The height of horses is given in hands. One hand is equivalent to 10cm or 4in.

Artist's note
Readers may care to note the original paintings from which the colour plates in this book
were prepared are available for private sale. All reproduction copyright whatsoever is
retained by the publisher. All enquiries should be addressed to:

Brian Delf
7 Burcot Park
Burcot
Abingdon
OX14 3DH
UK

The publishers regret that they can enter into no correspondence upon this matter.

The Woodland Trust
Osprey Publishing is supporting the Woodland Trust, the UK's leading woodland
conservation charity, by funding the dedication of trees.

www.ospreypublishing.com

BRONZE AGE WAR CHARIOTS

INTRODUCTION

You can put a person on a horse, but there is no guarantee that they will stay there. With the invention of the wheel, it became apparent to would-be equestrians that an animal harnessed to a vehicle lost most of its freedom of movement and so could be controlled. Besides, the floor of a vehicle must have seemed steadier and more comfortable than the bare back of a horse.

It seems more appropriate to say that the wheel evolved rather than to claim that it was invented (Piggott 1983: 39). Wheeled vehicles first appear around the fourth millennium BC within an area from the Rhine to the Indus. From the Late Funnel-Beaker culture (3100–2800 BC) of Bronocice (Poland) survives a cup incised with decoration including schematic plan views of four-wheeled wagons with draught poles and yokes. A ceramic model of the same date from Radošina (Czech Republic) has no wheels, but the foreparts of a pair of draught oxen. From Uruk level IVA (3200–3100 BC) in southern Mesopotamia come pictographic signs on inscribed clay tablets representing sledges with runners in front, as well as similar sledges raised over what may be either two rollers or four disc wheels. Finally, there are two cups, from the Baden-Pécel culture (2400–2200 BC) of Budakalász and Szigetszentmárton (Hungary), accurately modelled in the form of wagons with four disc wheels.

The realization of the wheel's formidable potential and the eventual domestication of the horse led to the most important new weapon of the Bronze Age, the war chariot. Little more than a mobile firing- or fighting-platform, the chariot had to offer speed and manoeuvrability

Qadesh relief, temple of Amun-Kamutef at Luxor. An Egyptian horseman, who wields a whip in his right hand, probably served as a mounted messenger. Note the rider sits far back, almost on the horse's croup. (Author's collection)

as well as stability for the firing or wielding of weapons. Unfortunately for the chariot-maker, these needs were contradictory. For speed and manoeuvrability were best provided by a small, lightweight vehicle. A stable firing- and fighting-platform, however, demanded a heavier vehicle, capable of supporting and providing operational space for at least one weapon-carrying warrior in addition to the charioteer. Despite these rival claims, however, the chariot finally evolved into a finely balanced war machine, serving both needs equally effectively. Yet all this depended on many prior developments – in metallurgy, woodworking, tanning and leatherwork, and the use of glues, bone and sinew – but above all on the domestication and improvement in physique of the wild horse.

CHRONOLOGY

The central debate surrounding the chronology for events in the Near East concerns certain observations of the planet Venus recorded in a Babylonian omen text, which gives us a choice between 'high', 'middle' and 'low' chronologies for the Bronze Age. By the high chronology, the regnal dates for Hammurabi of Babylon were 1848–1806 BC; by the middle chronology 1792–1750 BC and by the low chronology 1728–1686 BC. The middle chronology is followed for events in Mesopotamia. However, most Egyptologists tend to favour the low chronology for Egyptian history before 1000 BC. On the high chronology Rameses II's accession year was 1304 BC, on the middle chronology 1290 BC and on the low chronology 1279 BC. The low chronology is adopted for New Kingdom Egypt.

EARLY BRONZE AGE

Southern Mesopotamia	Egypt	Aegean
Late Uruk 3100–2900 BC	Early Dynastic 3000–2686 BC	Early Helladic (EH) 2900–2000 BC
Early Dynastic I 3000–2750 BC	Old Kingdom 2686–2181 BC	
Early Dynastic II 2750–2600 BC	First Intermediate Period 2181–2055 BC	
Early Dynastic III 2600–2350 BC		
Akkad I 2350–2150 BC		
Ur III 2150–2000 BC		

MIDDLE BRONZE AGE

Southern Mesopotamia	Egypt	Aegean
Isin-Larsa 2000–1600 BC	Middle Kingdom 2055–1650 BC	Middle Helladic (MH) 2000–1650 BC
Babylon I 1800–1600 BC	Second Intermediate Period 1650–1550 BC	

Northern Mesopotamia	Southern Mesopotamia	Egypt	Aegean
Old Assyrian Kingdom 1900–1400 BC	Kassite Dynasty 1600–1150 BC	New Kingdom 1550–1069 BC	Late Helladic (LH) 1650–1050 BC
Middle Assyrian Kingdom 1400–1050 BC			

In the Aegean, events must be dated by correlation with Egyptian and Mesopotamian chronology. In particular, the relative chronology supplied by Mycenaean pottery must fit into the absolute framework derived from Egypt. All dates are approximate and not absolute, and come almost entirely from two sources, namely radiocarbon dates and artefacts found in archaeologically sound Aegean contexts.

PROTO-PALATIAL PERIOD

LH I, IIA & IIB	Grave Circles A & B Mycenae	1650–1425 BC

PALATIAL PERIOD

LH IIIA & LH IIIB	Mycenaean palace complexes	1425–1200 BC
LH IIIB/C	Palace destruction levels	1200 BC

POST-PALATIAL PERIOD

LH IIIC		1190–1050 BC
Sub-Mycenaean	Transition to Iron Age	1050–1000 BC

THE HORSE

Though equipped with powerful jaws and even more powerful hindquarters, the horse seldom uses them as potential weapons, preferring discretion to valour. Yet throughout man's history the horse has been his most loyal and steadfast ally, especially in the arena of war. 'He smells the battle from afar, the thunder of captains and shouting' (Job 39:25), thus enabling these captains to carve out their empires. The horse, as the historian Franz Hancar so aptly defines him, is *das Geschichte machende Haustier*, the history-making animal.

Origins

As the soothsayer told the envoys of Croesus, king of Lydia, the horse is 'a warrior and a foreigner' (Herodotos 1.78), and it is as an invader that the horse arrived in the Near East. Wild horses were unknown in Mesopotamia, inhabiting only the open pasturage of the Eurasian steppe and semi-steppe of the Ukraine. Of the true horse two types are known for certain. The central Asian wild horse, known as Przewalski's,

The Standard of Ur is a double-sided panel from an Early Dynastic IIIA tomb (PC779) in the royal cemetery at Ur. The battle scene shows four-wheeled battlewagons equipped with quivers containing short spears. (British Museum, London, WA121201, photograph author's collection)

is yellow-dun in colour, with whitish under parts and standing around 13.2 hands high, it has narrow 'coffin' feet like an ass, a coarse head, thick neck and short, erect mane. The European wild horse, known as the tarpan, was mouse-grey or blue-dun in colour, with a black dorsal stripe and short, erect mane. It was similar in stature to a mule.

In the eighth millennium BC Neolithic man turned from hunting and occasional food gathering to the practice of cultivating cereal crops and the herding of animals. Among the first of the domesticated mammals, together with pigs and ovicaprids, were the larger and more powerful cattle, to be joined, much later, by horses.

The horse was probably first domesticated on the steppes above the Black Sea, where semi-sedentary herdsmen used horses, like their cattle, as a source of hide and food on the hoof. From the Srednij Stog culture of the Dnieper-Don the bones of apparently domesticated horses form the majority among those excavated from settlement sites dated to the fourth millennium BC. However, it remained an animal to be herded and eaten, rather than corralled and ridden.

Into Egypt

The peoples of the steppes kept no written records at this time, but their neighbours south of the mountain ranges did. In the third millennium BC the cuneiform clay tablets of Mesopotamia occasionally mention the horse under the name of *anše.kur.ra* ('ass of the mountains'), and this rather round-about way of expressing the horse indicates the scribes' comparative unfamiliarity with the animal (Pritchard 1969: 646, 647). Sumerian texts show the use of a generic equid Sumerogram, *anše*, which covered the ass and its hybrids, the onager and the horse. They were further distinguished by qualifying epithets in which, for instance, *anše.dun.gi* ('ass of the desert') meant ass or donkey.

Documentary evidence for the horse remains sparse until well into the second millennium BC. The Sumerogram for the horse then appears in Isin-Larsa and Old Babylonian texts from Mesopotamia and Elam, in Old Babylonian documents from Syria, and in Old Hittite sources from Hattusa-Bogazköy. These texts include literary works, such as hymns and animal proverbs, practicable texts on care and feeding, and diplomatic correspondence that mentions the exchange of horses and their role as valued gifts among monarchs.

The horse arrived too late for the Egyptians to include it in their pantheon of gods. Later, when Egypt became influenced by foreign cults, the horse was associated with the Canaanite goddess Astarte, and

Equus
The genus *equus* is divided into several distinct species. *Equus asinus*, the wild ass, was once indigenous to Sudan, Somalia and the Fertile Crescent, but is now restricted to Sudan and Somalia – preferring stony broken country or low hills. *Equus hemionus*, the onager, was hunted for its meat and hide and was also captured and managed in herds. The onager had a wide distribution from Syria to Turkmenia (now restricted to Iran and Turkestan), preferring the flat desert. Crossed with donkeys the onager gave a larger and stronger animal than either parent, the offspring being destined for draught work. *Equus ferus* can be divided into two sub-species, *equus ferus przewalskii* (Przewalski's horse) and *equus ferus gmelini* (tarpan). The domesticated horse, *equus caballus*, is descended from *equus ferus* and is distinguished from it by having 64 chromosomes, as against the 66 of surviving Przewalski's horses, but is otherwise a unitary sub-species.

became a favourite of charioteers as the 'mistress of mares'. Nevertheless, one of the names they used for the horse was 'the beautiful', which perhaps sums up the Egyptians' thoughts on encountering the animal for the first time. The earliest recorded find of a horse is that from Buhen, a Middle Kingdom fortress in Nubia.

The fortress was destroyed by fire during the turbulent period that preceded the seizure of Lower Egypt by the Hyksos (*c.*1650 BC), and the skeleton of a horse was found deposited on a walkway forming part of the mud-brick ramparts. Remarkable for its large size (15.2 hands), and for its slender build, the animal was a 19-year-old gelding afflicted with ringbone at the pasterns, which often causes lameness. It is clear a metal bit caused the excessive wear on the grinding teeth, perhaps indicating driving or riding use. The first direct reference to a horse-drawn chariot in Egypt is that of Ahmose (r.1550–1525 BC), the founder of Dynasty XVIII. One of his warriors, also named Ahmose, claims to have followed on foot the chariot of the pharaoh in the attack on Avaris (Tell ed-Dab'a), the Hyksos capital (Pritchard 1969: 554). Over the next three centuries their use in war became widespread, but always as draught animals for chariots and not as mounts for cavalry.

Driven, not ridden
The reason for this is twofold. The first decisive factor was the degree of domestication of the horse. Although the size of a horse does not have as great a bearing on its ability to carry weight as would first appear, its conformation does, and this also affects its durability. The more compact the animal, the greater its load-bearing capacity. At this date the horse was too slight, scrawny and narrow to be effective as a cavalry mount. For although the domesticated tarpan was infinitely better than the ass for galloping with a chariot in and out of battle, it did not have the strength to carry a man, particularly an armoured man, fast and far. Experiments with replicas of chariots demonstrate that chariot horses could cover some 10 to 14kmph at a trot, and gallop at speeds of 20 to 30kmph (Piggott 1992: 18).

The muscles used and the muscular effort exerted in carrying a load are quite different from those required to pull one. Draught animals harnessed to four-wheeled vehicles carry only the weight of the pole or shafts. Those hitched to two-wheeled vehicles may carry anything, from almost no weight to a certain portion of the vehicular load, depending on the position of the axle, the weight of the pole or shafts and the gradient of the terrain. The ridden animal, on the other hand, bears the full weight of the load.

Selective breeding, and more importantly, the switch from grass to grain feeding, eventually led to larger, stronger strains able to stand up to the rough life of a cavalry mount and the climate of the Near East – the Sumerian animal proverb, 'you sweat like a horse' (Gordon 1958: 19), being a reminder that the horse was a northern beast. This was only possible, however, in fertile, civilized countries with grain to spare. The horse-trainer Kikkuli of Mitanni (*fl.*1350 BC) specifies three cereal additives to hay: two grain types, wheat and barley, and meal and groats, as well as salt. In the *Odyssey*, Telemachos and his retinue unharnessed their chariot horses, leant the vehicles against the wall and 'put down fodder before them and mixed white millet with it' (4.41), while according to the Old Testament, barley and straw were provided for the horses of Solomon (1 Kings 4:28).

The horse may have been a less stable firing- or fighting-platform and more vulnerable than a chariot, but it had greater mobility and was tactically more flexible. Hence the gradual shift from chariotry to cavalry in Assyria. Tukulti-ninurta II (r.890–884 BC) is the first to record 'horse(men) [who go] at my side' (Luckenbill 1926: 1.406), that is, a mounted bodyguard as opposed to scouts or messengers, and mounted archers are widely depicted on the bronze-bound gates of Balâwât constructed under Shalmaneser III (r.858–824 BC). Yet the mounted archers of Shalmaneser's army still sit well back in the traditional 'donkey seat' manner, and each archer is accompanied by a second rider protecting him with a shield and apparently controlling the reins of both mounts. In other words, these paired warriors were still, in essence, part of the 'chariot-system'. The spear-armed horsemen of Tiglath-pileser

III (r.745–727 BC), although still shown in pairs, appear to sit more comfortably on their horses, with a good forward seat and naturally falling legs. His successor, Sargon II, was protected by 'one thousand fierce horsemen, bearers of bow, shield, and spear, my brave warriors, trained for battle' (Luckenbill 1927: 2.170, cf. 154).

Proto-horsemen

The first indication of horses being used without chariots is from an equestrian model dated to c.1350 BC. It represents an Egyptian clad only in a short kilt and completely unarmed, riding bareback on a horse controlled only by a single leather throng apparently tied around its lower jaw. A relief from the abandoned private tomb at Saqqara of general Horemheb, who reigned (1323–1295 BC) as the last of the Dynasty XVIII pharaohs, shows a similar horseman wielding a whip in his right hand. The reliefs commemorating Rameses' victory at Qadesh (1274 BC) provide another four examples of Egyptian horsemen, who are similarly dressed in kilts and head-cloths, and are variously equipped with quivers and bows. All have whips. One is shown riding side-saddle, while all four mounts wear a simple harness rather than the headstalls worn by chariot horses in the same reliefs.

None of these riders appear relaxed, comfortable or proficient. Sitting far back, almost on the horse's croup like a peasant on a donkey, they appear somewhat apprehensive, gripping nervously with knee and calf. The 'donkey seat' probably reflects time-honoured ass riding. This animal has very low withers, straight shoulders and a low head-and-neck carriage, so that the rider cannot adopt the 'control position' but has to sit back to avoid the sensation of going off over his mount's head. Such a seat is fairly comfortable at the gentle travelling gait of the ass. By comparison a horse has more prominent withers and a higher head carriage, which permit the adoption of the 'control position'. A rider seated on the croup receives the full shock of locomotion at a fast gait from the then very active hindquarters. The pounding of the rider's weight also abuses the mount's kidneys. As a consequence, the horse was quite unsuitable for any but the most lightly clad rider who was not pushing his mount too hard.

The primary purpose of these proto-horsemen was to act as messengers carrying despatches, or as scouts gathering vital intelligence. The official documents relating to Qadesh record that Rameses' vizier despatched a mounted messenger with orders to hasten laggard troops (Breasted 1927: 3.324, 334), while three of the four Egyptian horsemen depicted in the battle reliefs are specifically designated as *khapityu* ('scouts').

Bareback riding demanded its own set of skills, as the Greek soldier-scholar Xenophon (b. c.428 BC) makes abundantly clear in his manual of horsemanship. After explaining what the rider should do 'if he is to make the best of himself and his horse in riding' (*Peri Hippikis* 7.1), he describes the essential preliminary of 'sitting':

When he is seated, whether on bareback or on the cloth, we would not have him sit as if he were on his chair, but as though he were standing upright with his leg astride. For thus he will get a better grip of his horse with his thighs … The lower leg including the foot must hang lax and easy from the knee down. For if he keeps his leg stiff and should strike against anything, he may break it, whereas, a loose leg will recoil, whatever it encounters, without disturbing the position of the thigh at all. (*Peri Hippikis* 7.5–6)

To ride bareback at full gallop in a straight line, according to Hyland, 'is relatively easy for a *good* horseman', but 'the picture changes once the same rider is armed and armoured' (1990: 130).

There is a rather disparaging reference to horse riding from the palace archive that has survived at the city-state of Mari on the upper Euphrates. A letter from Bahdi-Lim to Zimri-Lim of Mari (r.1779–1761 BC) offers him the following advice: 'Let my lord not ride horses. Let him mount only chariots or mules and honour his kingly head' (Gordon 1958: 19). The mule appears to have been regarded as a more dignified (and safer) mount, and an earlier letter from the Mari archive talks of four envoys despatched by Rim-Sîn of Eshnunna (r.1822–1763 BC) with an important communiqué for Hammurabi of Babylon mounted on donkeys.

BATTLEWAGON

In the third millennium BC there were two types of chariot, or 'battlewagons' to be more precise: the two-wheeled and the four-wheeled. The two-wheeled battlewagon is the subject of Early Dynastic I models such as the copper replica of a 'straddle-car' found at Tell Agrab (Iraq Museum, Baghdad, 31389), or the terracotta model of a 'platform-car' found at Kish (Ashmolean Museum, Oxford, 1925.291). The earliest representation of the four-wheeled battlewagon is that on an Early Dynastic I pot from Khafajah. It appears in military contexts from the Early Dynastic III period, the notable examples being the Standard of Ur and the Vulture Stele.

Traction
Four equids, both onagers and donkeys or the resulting hybrids, provided draughts for these battlewagons. In the Early Dynastic II burials at Kish, Grave 2 contained a four-wheeled vehicle and four donkeys, while Grave 3 contained the remains of three similar vehicles and another pair of donkeys. From Lagash there is the Early Dynastic IIIB burial of a human and an equid, which was either a donkey or an onager. In comparable burials near Nippur, Abu Salabikh Grave 162 contained four donkeys buried in two pairs as if in harnessed teams. Near Baghdad, Tell Razuk Grave 12 held a pair lying in a similar position.

The fact that four such animals were required suggests that they were not very robust. It also suggests that the battlewagon was relatively heavy, and that its traction system did not fully exploit the haulage power of the draught team. The method

The Vulture Stele put up by Eanatum II of Lagash commemorates his victory over the people of Elam. On the bottom register the king leads his troops in a battlewagon. (Musée National du Louvre, Paris, AO16109, photograph Esther Carré)

Bowstrings were made of four strands of twisted gut. Arrows usually had a reed shaft, but were footed with hardwood and tipped with bronze. Drawn to the ear, thus fully stretching the sinew and compressing the horn, a composite bow had more power than a self-bow. This factor, combined with its shorter span, meant it was well suited for use in a chariot: 29 composite bows belonging to Tutankhamun (r.1336–1327 BC) vary in length from 1.07 to 1.4m. Furthermore, it could be kept strung for long periods without distortion or loss of power.

A combination of leg and manual force was the only possible method of stringing a composite bow. The archer would bend the bow between his legs and at the same time stoop down to fit the bowstring. From constant practice, the archer knew exactly how and when to apply the muscular force of leg and arm necessary to perform the operation successfully. If the limbs of the bow were given the slightest lateral twist as they were being bent, the horn parts were certain to splinter, and the bow was then useless and damaged beyond repair.

Tests using weapons from anthropological collections suggest that self-bows, not unlike the native Egyptian one, might attain a maximum range of 155 to 190m, and the oldest composite bows for which we have explicit data had an effective range of more than 175m. A replica of an angular composite bow, made by the anthropologist Saxton Pope, cast an arrow a distance of 230 to 260m on several occasions (McLeod 1970: 37).

of harnessing the team – as illustrated on two shell inlays from Mari (Musée National du Louvre, Paris, 2468, 451) – was by means of braided-rope neck straps, with the two inner animals under a yoke slightly shaped to fit their necks. The neck straps of this pair were fastened directly to the yoke, while those of the outer two were attached to it on one side only and with a little play. Control was achieved by means of a ring through the nasal cartilage, those of the outriggers being connected by a line only to the yoke. This arrangement allowed for braking only, with little or no directional control likely.

Wheel
Craftsmen had yet to succeed in placing the axle at the rear of the carriage on a two-wheeled battlewagon. This was no doubt due to the weight of the vehicle, as a rear axle tended to place the bulk of the load upon the shoulders of the draught animals. Stability was achieved by linking the wheels to a long axle-rod so that they were clear of the sides of the carriage. A four-wheeled battlewagon recovered from an Early Dynastic IIIA tomb in Kish has axles 90cm long, while the carriage has only a width of 45cm. The wheels themselves were all without exception heavy, solid, and without spokes. The diameters of those from battlewagons excavated at Ur, Kish and Susa vary from 50cm to 1.05m.

To give them greater strength, and to allow for a greater diameter, the wheels were made not of a single wooden plank but of three sections. These were bound together with external slats or ropes, dowelled together internally, and the whole consolidated with either a leather, reed or wood tyre secured by copper hobnails. These not only strengthened the wheel but also gave greater stability to the vehicle by acting as studs that gripped the ground.

Carriage
The carriage of the four-wheeled battlewagon was typically made from thin wooden struts backed with panels of wood or ox-hide. The carriage front was high enough to offer protection to the charioteer – suggesting that these battlewagons were employed mainly for direct assault on the enemy – though the sides were low. Indeed, there is no indication that the front axle was capable of pivoting, and even if it could, the degree of turn would be slight since the front wheels could not possibly have swung under the carriage. At the rear of the carriage was a small platform, which provided additional space for the warrior. This extension to the main platform enabled him to operate more freely without jostling the charioteer.

Armament
The battlewagon was armed with a quiver holding short spears. Occasionally, an axe or a sickle sword was also carried, the latter being a slashing weapon invented in Sumer at this time. The absence of the composite bow from the armament of the Sumerian warrior is more instructive, as it became the weapon of choice for the chariot warrior in the Late Bronze Age.

The absence of the bow demonstrates that the primary function of the Sumerian battlewagon was to charge and panic the enemy whilst the warrior engaged him with spears. Experiments have shown that an expert javelin-thrower can launch 30 javelins per minute at a distance of up to 60m from a replica battlewagon moving at a speed of 14 to 17kmph (Littauer and Crouwel 1979: 33). As the vehicle closed in, the warrior could resort to axe or sickle sword.

Two-wheeler

Although not normally equipped with weapons, these one-man vehicles undoubtedly served on the battlefield, if only for communications purposes. The straddle-car is not only the subject of the model from Tell Agrab, but also features on an Early Dynastic III relief from Ur (University of Philadelphia Museum, CBS17086).

Of simple construction, the two-wheel chariot consisted of an axle with two wheels, and a thick padded saddle on a vertical post set into the draught pole directly above the axle. The rider sat or stood astride the saddle with his feet either on the fixed axle or on rests directly in front of it. Thus his weight was placed directly over the axle where it would be in balance, and would ensure that the least load was placed on the necks of the team. During periods of speed he could stand just ahead of the axle fulcrum, stabilizing the vehicle with his weight and using his ankle, knee and hip joints as springs to absorb the jolting. He could also grip the saddle with his thighs and calves for greater security when necessary.

Not all of these vehicles were unarmed, however, for the Ur relief depicts a straddle-car equipped with a quiver housing short spears, which suggests a move away from four- and two-wheeled battlewagons to just two-wheeled battlewagons. In the Sumerian texts *mar-gid-da* is the term used for the four-wheeled wagon (Akkadian *eriqqu*), and *gigir* is a general all-purpose vehicle word, but especially one with two-wheels, the cuneiform character for which shows a stylized disc wheel.

The first representation of the composite bow is that carried by Naram-Sîn (r.2291–2255 BC) on his victory monument. Here, the Akkadian god-king triumphs over the Lullubi, a tribe of the Zagros foothills. (Musée National du Louvre, Paris, SB4, photograph Esther Carré)

PROTO-CHARIOT

Early in the second millennium BC the battlewagon underwent a revolutionary development that would turn this heavy compression-structure with solid disc wheels into an effective war machine. The development of steam-bent wood techniques not only allowed the construction of the spoked wheel with curved felloes, but also the manufacture of a light tension-structured chariot body. It would be this innovation that allowed the shifting of the single axle to the rear, which in turn made the chariot, as we can now properly call it, more manoeuvrable. Manoeuvrability was further enhanced by the use of the domesticated horse as a draught animal.

Construction

Diverse two-wheeled vehicles, which contributed different elements to the eventual chariot, are known from Syrian and Anatolian cylinder seals, as well as terracotta models from Mesopotamia.

One Anatolian seal from Karum level II at Kültepe shows a chariot with a low, open railing front and rear, while the impression of another Anatolian example has the cab railing extending along front and sides, with the rear open for quick mounting (Metropolitan Museum of Art, New York, 66.245.176). A fragmentary model from Uruk also demonstrates the latter, with the railings at hip height (Vorderasiatisches Museum, Berlin, A11576).

A seal of Hammurabi of Babylon (r.1792–1750 BC) depicts a modified platform-car with a traditionally shaped but lower front, very low side screens and a floor projecting to the rear of the cab supporting a seat with low arms (British Museum, London, 16815a). The chariot wheel is four-spoked and the draught team consists of two horses, harnessed and controlled in what appears to be a new manner.

Another example of the transitional vehicle comes from a Syrian seal, which illustrates a chariot with solid sides, perhaps basketry, and a charioteer who carries a quiver on his back (Ashmolean Museum, Oxford, 1920.25). Other Syrian impressions show the more advanced, steam-bent framework: one seal shows a ruler equipped as an archer in a horse-drawn chariot escorted by footmen (Ashmolean Museum, Oxford, 1912.115).

Horse-drawn

One of the earliest references to the horse is in a hymn of self-praise by Shulgi of Ur (r.2094–2047 BC). The king boasts of the speed of his day's journey of 15 'double-hours' – roughly 140km – from Nippur to Ur as equal to that of a donkey, a mule and a 'horse with a waving tail' (Pritchard 1969: 585, 586). Shulgi also claimed the hero Gilgamesh as his brother, and in the *Epic of Gilgamesh* there is an early allusion to the horse-drawn chariot: 'Your horses shall run proud at the chariot' (Tablet VI.i).

Yet it is evidence from the Mari archive that confirms these proto-chariots were horse-drawn. A despatch from Shamsi-adad I of Assyria (r.1813–1781 BC) to his son Iasmah-adad, the governor of Mari, concerns the horse-drawn chariots that will take part in the forthcoming New Year festivities (Oppenheim 1967: 109). There is also the Mesopotamian fable, the *Story of the Horse and the Ox*. In this tale the Horse points out his usefulness to the Ox who, in reply, states that he too contributes to a success in battle since the quivers and harness are made from his hide. The Horse quickly retorts, boasting of his pleasant life, how he is lodged near the king and the great men, how choice and varied his food is, and that his flesh is not eaten.

Traction

The seal impressions show a significant change in harnessing technique. Instead of the inefficient halters of the Sumerian type, a wooden 'yoke saddle' was used so that the main effort of traction was taken on the horse's shoulders. Resembling an inverted Y, the legs lay across the horse's shoulders just in front of the withers, and towards the end of each leg was a hole through which passed the ends of a neck strap that kept the yoke saddle in place. A girth band similarly fastened to the ends of the yoke saddle and passed under the horse's belly just behind the forelegs, enabling the chariot to be reversed.

Slightly later Egyptian representations show that chariot teams were controlled either by a bitted bridle or by a fitted headstall. The four reins – two per horse – were attached either to the ends of the mouthpiece of the bit or to the left and right sides of the noseband of the headstall. The reins were carried back to the loops on the horses' shoulders near the ends of the yoke saddles (Littauer and Crouwel 1985: 102). Two main categories of metal bit were current in the Near East at this time, namely the bar snaffle with circular cheek pieces, and the broken snaffle with long, rectangular cheek pieces (Littauer and Crouwel 1979: 86–90).

EGYPTIAN CHARIOT

Under the pharaohs the chariot (*wereret* or *merkebet*, a Canaanite loan word) was a formidable weapon. Lightweight, manoeuvrable and stable, it was drawn by two stallions. On the basis of surviving yokes it appears that the average height of a chariot team was around 13.2 hands. The crew comprised a charioteer-cum-shield-bearer and a lightly armoured warrior equipped with a composite bow, short spears and a hefty sidearm of bronze, the *khopesh*.

Beginnings
'I will take over chariotry' was the boast of the Theban pharaoh, Kamose (r.1555–1550 BC), as he set out to break the rule of the Hyksos king, Apepi (Pritchard 1969: 554). However, it was left to his younger brother and the founder of Dynasty XVIII, Ahmose, to complete the expulsion of the Hyksos and thus launch what we know as the New Kingdom period of Egyptian history. Yet Kamose, braggart though he may have been, was shrewd enough to see the potential advantages of incorporating the chariot into an army based exclusively on the unarmoured foot-warrior.

Introduced into Egypt by the Hyksos (the Greek rendering of the Egyptian term *heka khaswt*, 'rulers of foreign lands'), the horse-drawn chariot had played an important part in the task of reducing Lower Egypt to vassaldom. As a result of the successful struggle against the Hyksos, Ahmose and his successors, particularly the warrior-pharaohs Thutmose III (r.1479–1425 BC) and Rameses II (r.1279–1213 BC), were able to forge an elite chariot corps, the primary striking arm of an army that was to spearhead Egyptian expansion into Retennu (*rtnw*, the Egyptian term for Syria-Palestine) and Nubia.

Development
Prior to Thutmose IV (r.1400–1390 BC), Egyptian chariots were of lightweight design – witness the

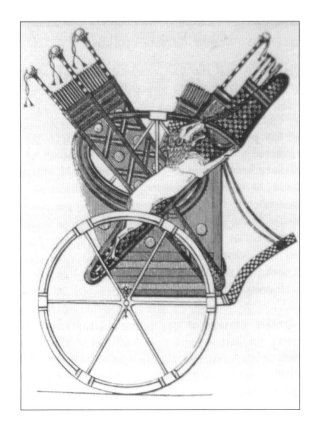

Egyptian chariot, with bow-case and weapon cases – the bow-case is placed in an inclined position, pointing forwards with the mouth level with the archer's right hand. (Reproduced from J. Gardner Wilkinson, *The Ancient Egyptians: Their Life and Customs*, John Murray, London, 1854)

chariot being manhandled by a Syrian tribute bearer in a wall painting from the tomb of Rekhmira at Thebes (TT100) – having evolved little from those of their Hyksos and Canaanite mentors. By the end of his reign Egyptian chariots had assumed a more native style, with various types of imported hardwood, chosen for their qualities of strength and flexibility, being employed in their construction.

By Dynasty XIX the chariot had reached a peak of efficiency. This is evident from a relief in the mortuary temple of Rameses II, the Ramesseum, which portrays the warrior-pharaoh charging through the Hittites, his bow at the draw. His chariot has six-spoked wheels and its cab is generally heavier and more robust. With the axle set at the very rear of the body, the vehicle has optimum manoeuvrability and stability. Besides the bow-case, two extra weapon cases, both with arrows and two short spears, have increased the firepower. Each horse is wearing barding in the form of a textile trapper reinforced with bronze scales.

Construction

The cab of an early Dynasty XII chariot from Thebes is 1m wide, 50cm deep and 75cm high (Museo Archeologico, Florence). The axle is 1.5m wide and the four-spoked wheels are 80cm in diameter. The only provision for weaponry was the bow-case attached to the cab. While comparable in design, the cab of Tutankhamun's chariot A1 is heavier and more robust, and measures 1m in width and 1.25m in height (Egyptian Museum, Cairo, JE61990). The axle is 1.75m wide and the six-spoked wheels are 90cm in diameter. Extra weapon cases were to be added under Seti I (r.1294–1279 BC).

The cab was a steam-bent frame of ash or elm covered with ox-hide. To increase lightness the cover was only stretched over the front of the cab, leaving a large 'fenestration' at each side. The cab was fully open at the rear and wide enough to allow the two-man crew to stand side by side. The floor was D-shaped in plan and constructed out of rawhide thongs that passed through slots cut in the floor frame; they were interwoven to provide a flexible and strong surface that acted as a form of suspension in an otherwise unsprung vehicle.

Qadesh relief, Pylon I (South), the Ramesseum at Thebes, showing Rameses crushing the 'wretched Hatti' under the hooves of his chariot team. This motif emphasizes the might of the warrior-pharaoh as leader of the chariotry. (Author's collection)

The chariot had a simple sub-frame with a single, heat-bent draught pole, usually of elm and some 2.5m in length, sandwiched between the rear-mounted axle and the two grooved mountings that connected the axle to the sides of the floor frame. The draught pole thus ran beneath the centre of the floor, being secured by rawhide thongs to the front of the floor frame, before curving upwards to support a yoke, usually of willow.

Cut from elm (felloes, hub), ash (felly-bands) and almond or plum (spokes), the wheels were large and six-spoked. The spokes were composed of six steam-bent pieces of wood that were formed into a V-shape. These were then glued together in such a way that every spoke was composed of two halves of two V-shaped pieces, each V-tip being fastened to the hub by wet cattle intestines, which hardened as they dried. The rim was formed of four felloes bound to four felly-bands by strips of birch-bark-covered rawhide. A bronze wire passed through holes in the felloe and then wound around the felly-band for added security. At the same time, the wire held the butt ends of the felloes together. Rawhide tyres were shrunk over the wheels to stabilize the composite construction. Each wheel was attached to the axle by a small-lynch pin and secured by a thong that passed through the lower end.

Fashioned from ash or tamarind and covered with birch-bark, the axle was set as far back as possible to balance the vehicle and to improve speed and manoeuvrability. Being much longer than the width of the cab, the resulting wide wheel track gave the vehicle greater stability on sharp turns and provided good shock absorption.

Organization

Apart from its value as state-of-the-art military technology, the chariot was of paramount socio-political significance since it heralded the appearance of a chariot-warrior group, skilled fighters who monopolized the use of their specialized and extremely expensive vehicles. This new warrior aristocracy modelled itself on the ubiquitous Asiatic military elite known to the Egyptians as the *maryannu* ('young heroes').

The basic unit of the chariotry was the vehicle itself, driven by a charioteer-cum-shield-bearer (*kedjen*, 'charioteer', often called a *ger'iu*, 'shield-bearer'). The other occupant was the *seneny* (chariot warrior),

An Egyptian chariot in detail on the Qadesh relief, temple of Rameses II at Abydos. Note the bow-case and the weapon case for housing additional arrows and a pair of short spears. (Author's collection)

armed not only with composite bow and short spears, but also with a variety of side arms, such as dagger, mace, battle-axe or *khopesh.*

In addition to the shield carried by the charioteer, personal protection for the chariot warrior consisted of a textile corselet (multiple layers of linen impregnated with resin) or a scale corselet (bronze or hardened leather). Corselets were three-quarter or half-length, many offering additional protection to the wearer's neck. Headgear, if worn, included high-crowned bronze helmets and close-fitting scale 'hairpiece' caps. Attached to each chariot was a *peherer* (runner) armed with small shield and light-spear, warriors who fought on foot in support of the vehicle. Presumably especially athletic men were picked for this task.

Ten chariots formed a troop of chariotry under a *kedjen-tepy* (first charioteer). Five 'troops' formed a squadron under a 'standard-bearer of the chariot warriors'. Bellicose titles were given to these units, and the biography of Merenptah (r.1213–1203 BC) describes service as a prince, in squadrons named 'the Phoenix' and 'Manifest-in-Justice', which suggests that they were the basic tactical and administrative unit. The Abu Simbel relief illustrating Rameses' camp at Qadesh indicates that various administrative personnel were attached, which included an adjutant, stable-master, various scribes, grooms and artisans. Several squadrons could be combined to form a *pedjet* (host), led by a *hery-pedjet* (host-chief).

Deployment

On the Qadesh relief at Abu Simbel a body of Egyptian chariotry is shown in line abreast charging towards a similar line of Hittite chariots. Undoubtedly the Egyptians are attempting to inflict as many casualties as possible using long-range arrows and short-range spears, and, lacking the thrusting spear, are keen to avoid direct combat.

To prevent the likelihood of contact with the enemy, chariots would be well spaced to enable evading manoeuvres. For the Egyptians, quick turns at speed were the surest method of survival in chariot battle. Ideally, of course, if they could force their opponents to flinch and thus break off, they could then inflict heavy casualties from archery during the pursuit. The main disadvantage to them would have been the danger of being swept away by heavier opponents in the initial charge.

Essentially the Egyptian chariot was a mobile archery-platform. One document notes the departure of a chariot for Retennu with a well-stocked quiver of 80 arrows (Papyrus Koller I 1–2), while an account of the prowess of Amenhotep II (r.1427–1400 BC) at archery provides a crucial insight into chariotry training methods:

> He entered into his northern garden and found that there had been set up for him four targets of Asiatic copper of one palm in their thickness, with 20 cubits between one post and its fellow. Then His Majesty appeared in a chariot like Montu in his power. He grasped his bow and gripped four arrows at the same time. So he rode northward shooting at them like Montu in his regalia. His arrows had come out of the back thereof while he was attacking another post. (Pritchard 1969: 244)

This suggests that the emphasis was to train chariot warriors to fire with the horses at full gallop. It took a great deal of practice to reach this level of skill, as well as remarkable hand-to-eye co-ordination. However, while the warrior concentrated on shooting, the charioteer put his mind on driving the fast-moving vehicle, an equally demanding task.

Integral to the organization of the chariotry were the runners, who, as the name suggests, were expected to try to keep pace with the chariotry. However, they could also perform several tactical roles, such as screening the chariotry, following up a charge to despatch or capture fallen enemy crewmen, and rescuing wounded friendly crewmen. There are several reliefs that show runners in action. At Medinet Habu a line of spear-armed runners are shown operating on the flanks of a line of chariotry, while at Abydos runners are seen killing or cutting the hands off Hittite crewmen who have fallen from their vehicles. Interestingly,

Hittite chariots launching an attack as depicted on the Qadesh relief, temple of Rameses II at Abydos. Note the characteristic shape of the shield – rectangular with convex edges on the top and bottom, and concave edges on the sides. (Author's collection)

there are a few figures in these reliefs with bows instead of short spears, who could be crewmen from destroyed vehicles, who would join the runners in the midst of combat.

HITTITE CHARIOT

The Hittite chariot is known primarily through the Qadesh reliefs, which depict a number of vehicles whose axle passes beneath the centre of a heavy box-shaped cab. In some cases, however, there is no apparent distinction between Hittite and Egyptian chariots, as both have axles situated at the rear of the body base and cabs of steam-bent wood covered with stretched fabric or ox-hide. Of course it is impossible to determine the measure of accuracy of the Egyptian artists, but the variety of designs probably reflects the different client states of the Hittite empire from which chariot contingents were drawn.

A Hittite chariot, with the axle placed at the rear of the cab, possibly reflecting the various regions of the empire from which chariot contingents were drawn. (Qadesh relief, temple of Rameses II at Abydos, photograph author's collection)

Construction

It is significant that the more robust examples have their axles set further forward than was the norm in Syria, Canaan and Egypt. These 'heavy' chariots represent the 'Anatolian type', from the heart of the Hittite empire; they were crewed by three men whose combined weight would have made impractical the placement of an axle at the rear of the vehicle. Six-spoked wheels were standard, as is clear from the actual reliefs, and not eight as claimed by some scholars. This error has arisen because the Qadesh relief in the Ramesseum was erroneously copied and then widely reproduced in many books.

These bronze armour scales would have been sewn in rows onto a backing material such as linen or leather. Note each plate (c.6 x 1.5cm) has a reinforcing central spine. (Royal Museum, Edinburgh, photograph Esther Carré)

As with the Egyptian chariot, the frame, wheels, draught pole and yoke of the Hittite chariot were probably made from a variety of wood types. Judging from the Qadesh reliefs, the cab of the heavier chariot model looks as if it is constructed from slats of wood. Likewise, the draught pole disappears under the cab and probably continues to the rear of the cab for strength of construction. The axle is set beneath the centre of the cab, directly under the floor, again adding to its strength of construction. Like the Egyptian chariot, the floor was made up of interlaced rawhide thongs. The probable dimensions of the cab were about 1.25m in width, about 1m deep and slightly less than 1m high. The extra width and depth to the cab, which was possibly rectangular in plan, allowed it to accommodate the extra crewman.

Crew

The three-man crew consisted of an unshielded charioteer, a shield-bearer who doubled as a spearman, and an unshielded warrior armed with a thrusting spear. The first two wore lightweight textile armour, the third a high-crowned bronze helmet and three-quarter-length scale armour. Side weapons included sword, axe and mace. Hittites normally wore their hair in long pigtails or scalp locks, and in the Qadesh inscriptions Rameses II disparagingly refers to the Hittite charioteers as *humty* ('women-warriors').

Deployment

The robust Hittite chariot was well suited for close-quarter combat. The Hittite chariot teams in the Qadesh reliefs are usually shown as unarmoured, but a scene from the temple of Rameses II at Abu Simbel illustrates horse armour. In the style similar to that formerly employed by the Mitanni, this equine protection takes the form of a scale barding worn over a textile trapper, with a covering of studded fabric around the head.

Tactics were firmly based on the chariot's aggressive use in battle. One option, terrain permitting, would be a mass onslaught of chariots, preferably despatched before the opponent could properly deploy his forces. Against enemy chariotry the Hittite chariots would opt to charge into contact, aiming to thrust at their opponents with their spears. In the mêlée the heavier weaponry and more numerous crew would tell against

lighter chariotry, although Hittite chariots, with their centrally placed axle, were less manoeuvrable. Yet the third crewman meant the vehicle could afford to lose a man without becoming ineffective.

Essentially the Hittite chariot was a mobile fighting-platform, 'being', as Rameses explains, 'three men to a span, acting in unison' (Breasted 1927: 3.312). However, the ancient historians Littauer and Crouwel (1983: 187–192) argue that a warrior could not have thrust with a spear from a speeding chariot. For this reason Drews suspects that the Hittite chariot warrior used this weapon only against enemy infantry 'or chariot crewmen who had fallen to the ground' (1995: 116). He says 'Hittite chariot warriors were bowmen', their vehicles being used as mobile firing-platforms (1995: 121).

Early Hittite chariots had carried two men, the *kartappu* (charioteer), who doubled as a shield-bearer, and a *šuš* (warrior), armed with a composite bow. By the time of Qadesh, however, spears had been added, as had a third man. This may explain why the Egyptians were able to extricate themselves from potential defeat. The Hittite chariotry at

Qadesh would have represented a wide range of chariot tactics, varying from the skirmishing tactics of Syria-Palestine to the close-combat techniques of the Anatolia-Aegean area.

MYCENAEAN CHARIOT

The history of the Mycenaean chariot can be divided into two phases. The first belongs to the period 1550–1300 BC (LH I-IIIA) when the chariot took the form of a closed frame box design, the 'box-chariot'. The second coincides with the period 1300–1200 BC (LH IIIB) when chariot design had changed dramatically with the development of the 'rail-chariot'. The shift from box-chariot to rail-chariot marks the transition from a purely mobile fighting vehicle to a battlefield transport at a time when the Mycenaean world was in a state of fragmentation and dissolution.

Numbers
No recognizable parts of a Mycenaean chariot have been brought to light, but the Linear B 'chariot' tablets from Knossos list approximately 550 chariot bodies and at least as many pairs of wheels (Sc series). Similarly, at Pylos tablets list at least 200 pairs of wheels, as well as wood for the construction of 150 axles (Sa series), and two specifically mention

The Linear B clay tablets from the Mycenaean palaces provide inventories of helmets, body armour, weapons, chariot parts and horses, among other commodities. The term for chariot was *iqija*, for horse *i-qo*. (Author's collection)

chariot makers (En 421, 809). In addition, the tablets reveal that the wheels and bodies were manufactured in workshops adjacent to the palace, and stored in arsenals (Sa 02, Sb 1315, Sf 4428, So 0430, 894).

It seems that the ruler of a well-organized Mycenaean kingdom was able to field a chariot arm, albeit on a much smaller scale than the chariot kingdoms of the Near East. As we shall see, after his victory at Megiddo Thutmose III counted no fewer than 900 chariots amongst the booty taken from the warlords of Qadesh and Megiddo. Requiring the services of a large number of specialists – besides the privileged elite of chariot warriors and charioteers, horse trainers, grooms, veterinarians, and craftsmen were also vital – chariot forces were notoriously expensive to maintain. The rulers of Knossos and Pylos devoted a fair proportion of their resources to the maintenance of a chariotry of several hundred vehicles, and so it is no great surprise to find the chariot often depicted in Mycenaean art.

Box-chariot

Once introduced into the Mycenaean world, the chariot soon began to differ in terms of design from the Near Eastern type. The four-spoked wheel remains standard throughout this period – it was to be a feature of the rail-chariot also – but it was made stronger and more robust. The axle was positioned near the centre of the cab, and a shaft running horizontally from the yoke to the front of the cab further strengthened the vehicle. A wooden support joined this shaft to a curved draught pole that continued to the rear of the cab for strength of construction. It is possible that the shaft extended backward within the cab and curved round to join the floor, providing a partition and means of support for the crewmen. The cab itself was framed in steam-bent wood and either covered with ox-hide or wickerwork, with the floor probably consisting of interwoven rawhide thongs as in Near Eastern chariots. The woodwork was commonly of elm, willow, yew, boxwood and cypress. A Linear B tablet reads 'five pairs of wheels of elm wood, of better class, with tyres' (So 4437).

These are all features specifically designed to increase the strength of the vehicle. Whereas in Egypt the emphasis was on lightness because of

23

A box-chariot depicted on a tomb stele (LH I-IIB) from Shaft Grave V, Grave Circle A, Mycenae. The chariot warrior, apparently armed with a thrusting spear, pursues a fleeing foe. (National Archaeological Museum, Athens 1428, photograph author's collection)

the desire for speed and manoeuvrability over flat open terrain, the Mycenaean chariot was clearly a more robust vehicle intended to take the strain and bumps of close combat over broken ground.

Crew

The box-chariot was crewed by two men, a charioteer and a warrior, collectively known as *equeta* (followers). Battle-gear for the better-equipped warrior may have been similar to the Dendra panoply (LH IIIA), a remarkable suit of armour found in a chamber tomb at Dendra, near Argos. This is the only intact example discovered to date, though parts of another have been found at Thebes and the Dendra panoply appears often as an ideogram on Linear B tablets from Knossos (Sc series), Pylos (Sh series) and Tiryns (Si series).

Worn beneath the panoply, a quilted linen tunic made ideal padded protection. This would have softened blows and offered a degree of protection from the armour itself, which could be pushed into the flesh when damaged in combat. The less well-equipped charioteer wore a similar tunic. He also wore greaves of stiffened fabric, probably linen. They frequently appear in palace frescoes, even on otherwise lightly equipped troops.

Fragments of a boars' tusk helmet were discovered with the Dendra

panoply. This helmet type was constructed from plates of horn sliced

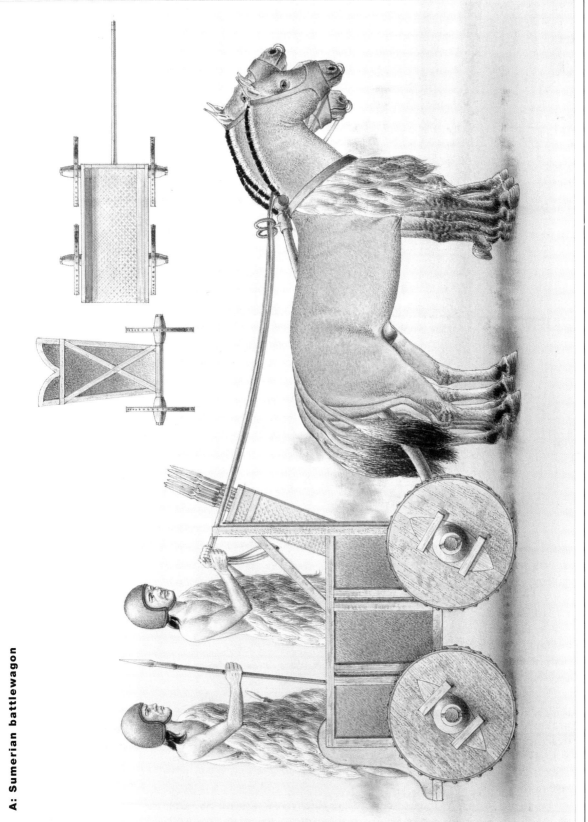

A: Sumerian battlewagon

B

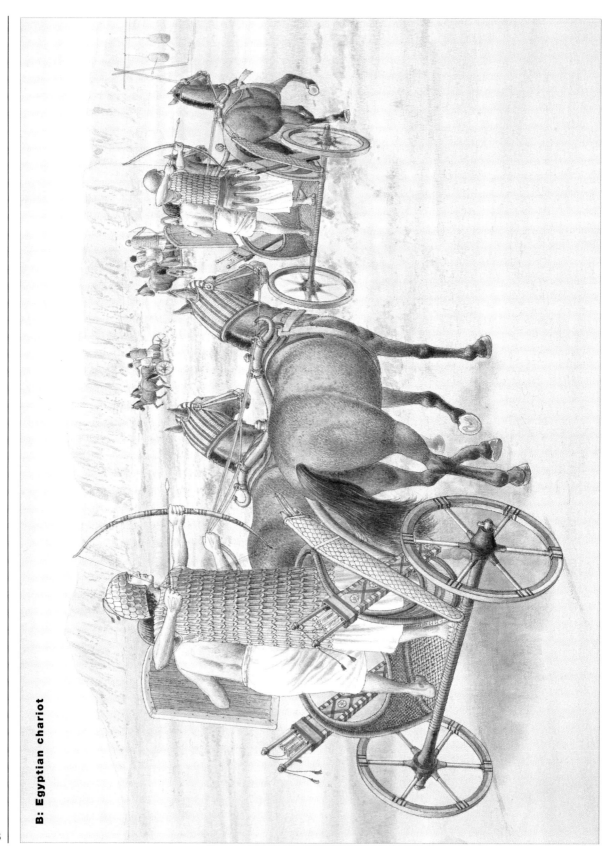

B: Egyptian chariot

D: Mycenaean box-chariot

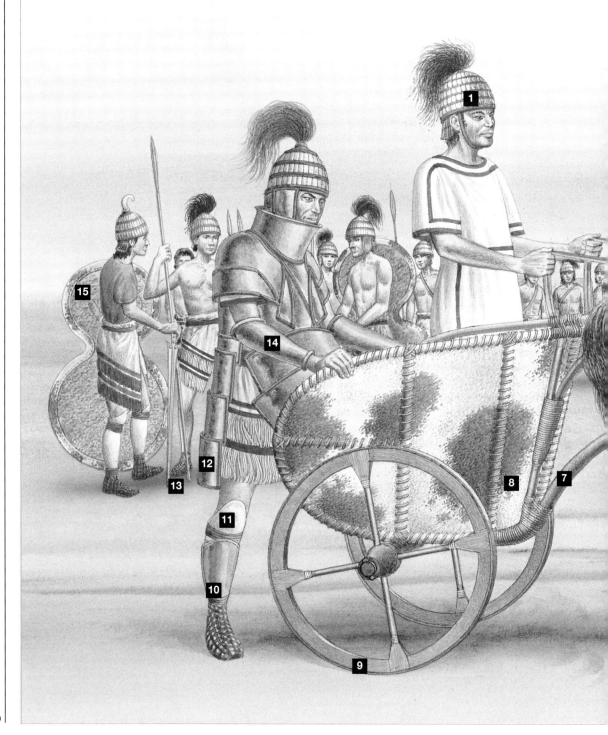

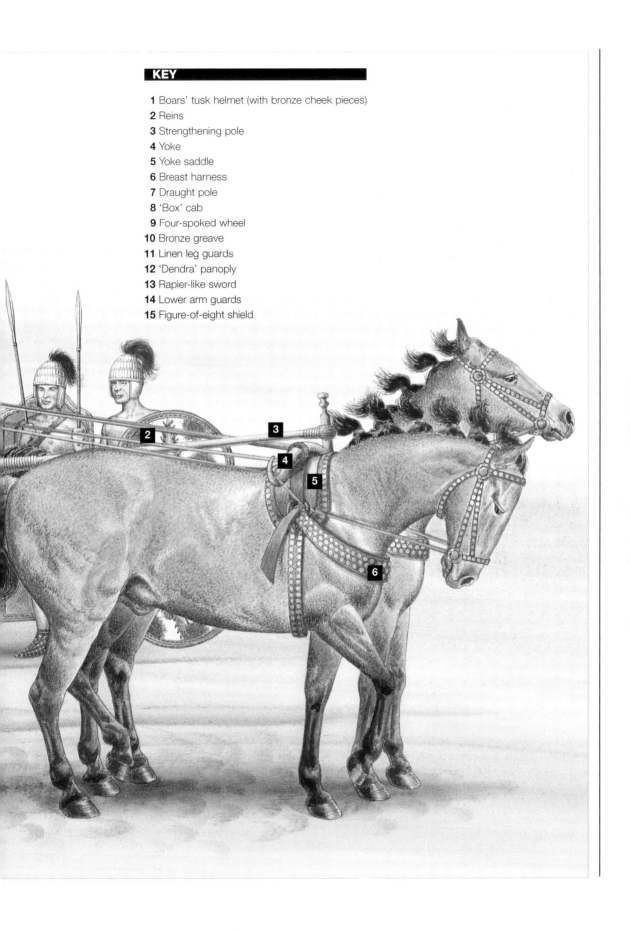

KEY

1 Boars' tusk helmet (with bronze cheek pieces)
2 Reins
3 Strengthening pole
4 Yoke
5 Yoke saddle
6 Breast harness
7 Draught pole
8 'Box' cab
9 Four-spoked wheel
10 Bronze greave
11 Linen leg guards
12 'Dendra' panoply
13 Rapier-like sword
14 Lower arm guards
15 Figure-of-eight shield

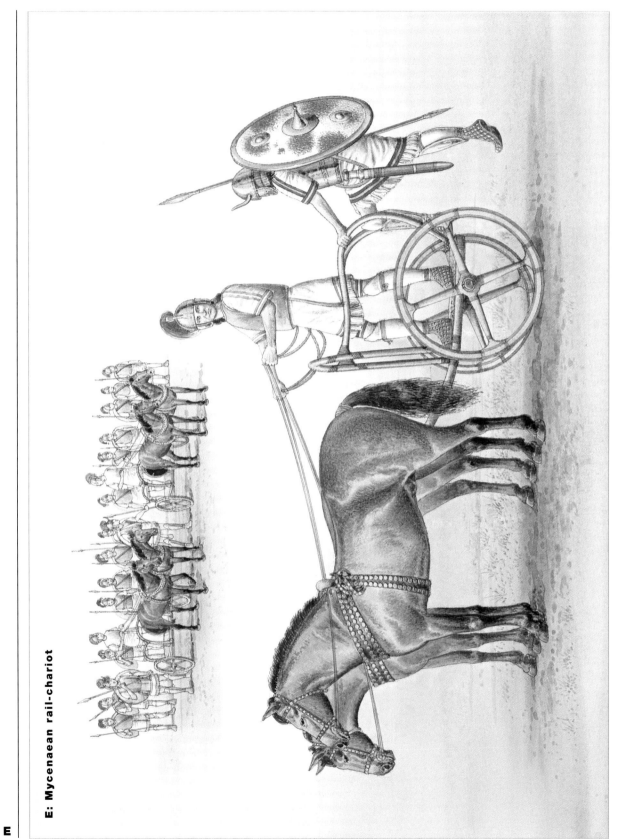

E: Mycenaean rail-chariot

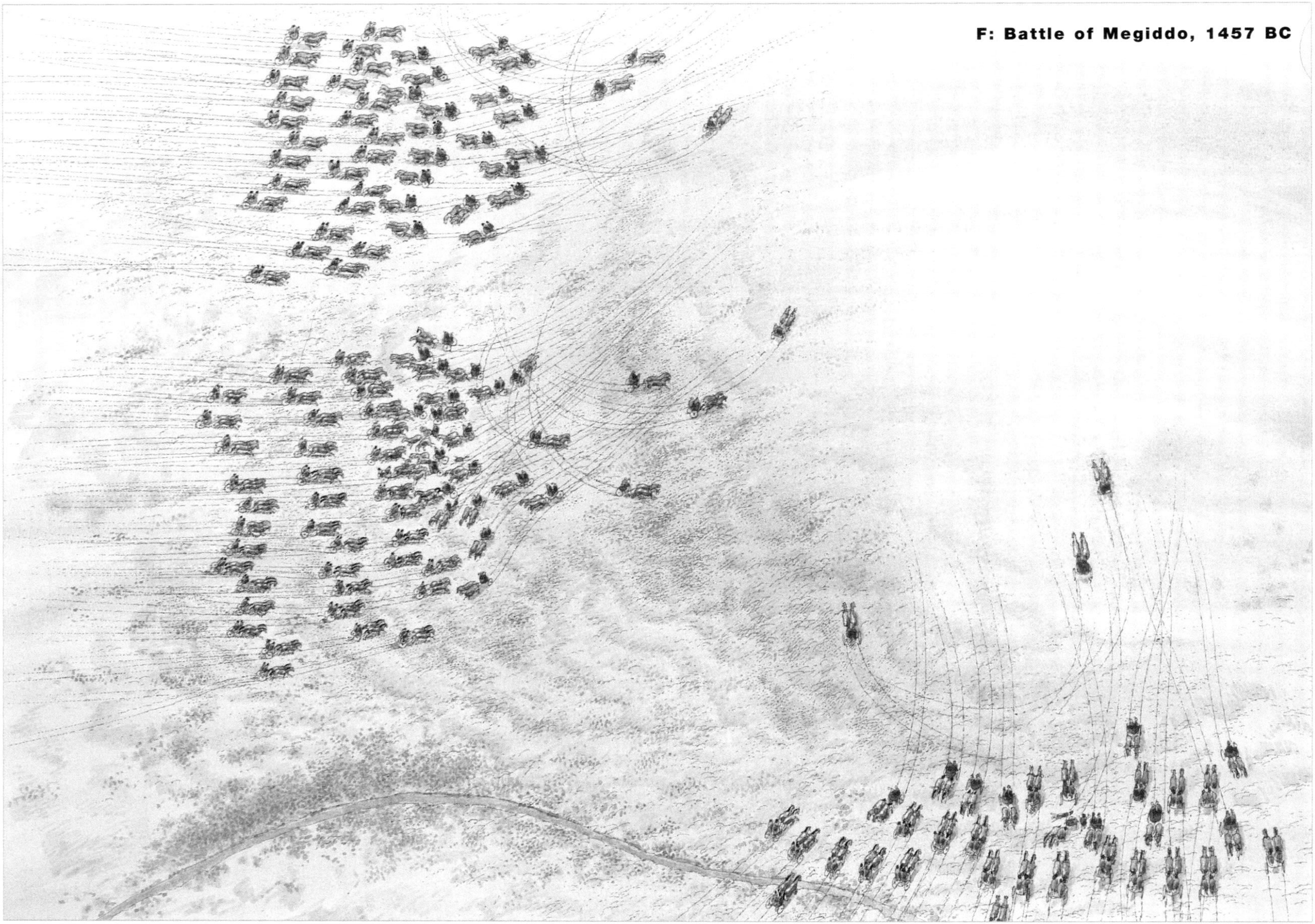

F: Battle of Megiddo, 1457 BC

F

G: Chariot clash at Qadesh, 1274 BC

The Dendra panoply (LH IIIA), recovered from a chamber tomb. Made of beaten sheet-bronze, this body armour was too rigid and cumbersome (not to mention extremely heavy and hot) for a foot-warrior to wear. (Archaeological Museum, Nauplion T12, photograph author's collection)

Dendra panoply

Made from 15 pieces of beaten sheet-bronze, the panoply is a tubular suit of armour that extends from chin to knees. The cuirass is of two parts, front and back plates, hinged together on the left side and secured by a single loop and slot on the right side. Similar loops on each shoulder allow for the attachment of shoulder guards. These have triangular plates that cover the warrior's armpits when his arms are in the raised position. There is also a high neck guard. The Linear B ideogram depicting the panoply makes the neck guard clearly discernible, and protection by a high bronze collar was a typical feature of Near Eastern armour as, for example, that illustrated in a wall painting from the Theban tomb (TT93) of the Dynasty XVIII high official Kenamun. Three pairs of curved plates hang from the waist to protect the groin and the thighs. All pieces are backed with leather and were loosely fastened by rawhide thongs to allow some degree of movement. The warrior also wore bronze lower-arm guards and greaves, as fragments of these were found alongside the panoply.

from boars' tusks and bound to a leather base with rawhide thongs. The Dendra helmet had bronze cheek pieces instead of the more usual horn type as depicted in palace frescoes. During the siege of Troy Homer often refers to flashing bronze helmets with horsehair plumes nodding above them (*Iliad* 5.681, 6.469-470, cf. 3.316), but only one complete bronze helmet has been discovered to date. From a burial in the North Cemetery at Knossos (LH IIIA), this helmet consists of a cap with a cast-bronze crest knob and two cheek pieces.

Armament for a chariot warrior consisted of a thrusting spear, and a side arm comprising a rapier-type sword, some 60cm in length, with a strong mid-rib. Requiring skill in use, this 'rapier' was a suitable weapon for inserting between the plates of an adversary's armour. In Grave Circle A at Mycenae many swords of this type were found along with a smaller number of spearheads remarkable for their large size – some 65cm long. Such heads can only have been attached to a thrusting weapon, not a throwing weapon, and wielded two-handed by a chariot-borne warrior, as depicted, possibly, on the stele from Shaft Grave V (LH I-IIB) and a sardonyx gemstone from Vaphio (LH IIB).

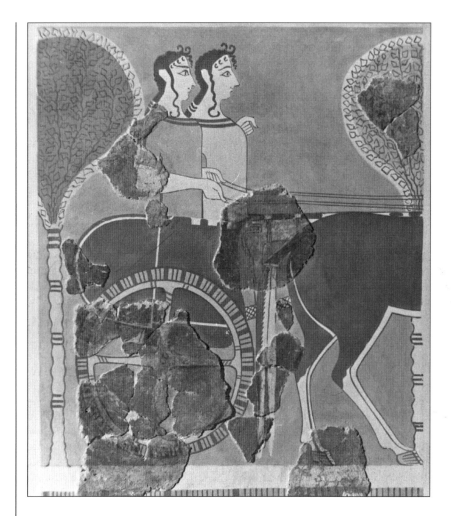

Fresco (LH IIIB) from the palace of Tiryns depicting a box-chariot. The frame is covered in a red hide or fabric cover, and the Linear B tablets mention red hides and crimson (*ponikija*) chariots. (National Archaeological Museum, Athens, photograph author's collection)

The Dendra panoply is clearly designed to deflect thrusts. A warrior engaging in combat from a chariot is in no position to wield a shield and thus he either has to rely upon the services of a shield-bearer, as did the Hittite warrior, or shield-bearer-cum-charioteer, as did the Egyptian warrior. Alternatively, he could encase himself in bronze armour.

Organization

The Linear B tablets also provide information concerning the possible military organization of a Mycenaean kingdom. At the very pinnacle of society was the warrior-king or *wanax* (Na 334, 1356, Ta 711, cf. Un 718), and immediately beneath him was the *lawagetas* (An 724, Un 219, 718). The *lawagetas* is a position variously interpreted as a war chief, whose duty it was to lead the host in battle and who was elected for that purpose, or as a prince learning the art of state craft through the role of commander-in-chief of the palace army. A later Germanic parallel exists for an elected war chief in times of hostilities (Tacitus, *Germania* 7.1), while a contemporary Hittite parallel exists for the idea of a prince commanding. Hattusilis III relates the following: 'When my father Mursilis became god, my brother Muwatallis seated himself on the throne of his father; and before the face of my brother I became chief of the armed forces' (*Apology of Hattusilis* I 22–24).

A krater shard (LH IIIB) from Tiryns depicting a rail-chariot containing two crewmen and a foot-warrior (possibly a runner). All are shown wearing body armour, perhaps bronze-reinforced corselets. (National Archaeological Museum, Athens, 1509, photograph author's collection)

Next came the *tereta* (Am 826, Ed 411, Uf 839) who were fief-holders owing some sort of feudal service to the *wanax*, who in turn held feudal obligation over lesser chieftains or *moroppas* who held a 'share of land' (Ag 64, An 519, Jo 438). A more prestigious title was that of *equeta* (Sa 789, 790). These men apparently had a military function, as they possessed chariots, although there may have been those who were not of such companion status since some items of chariot equipment are listed in the tablets as 'suitable for followers' (Sa 709, 787, cf. So 4437), implying that the best equipment was the preserve of the *equeta*.

Many tablets deal with the muster of chariots or parts of chariots, indicating that the palace closely supervised the readiness of the chariot arm. Only those chieftains providing a complete vehicle are mentioned by name, otherwise the tablets list the relevant vehicle parts from those chieftains who could only furnish incomplete chariots (Sc 226, 238, Sd 9422 [chieftains], Sa 487, Sf 0420, So 0430 [parts]). It would seem that the *tereta* were chieftains who provided a feudal host, which included both foot soldiers and their own personal retinue consisting of chariots; poorer and lesser chieftains, the *moroppas*, furnished the palace armoury with chariot parts, while the chariot-owning *equeta* formed the elite chariotry.

Deployment

A Mycenaean chariot battle would have resembled that experienced in the Near East, albeit on a smaller scale. As the chariots advanced into contact they would initially keep in formation (probably in line abreast), the gaps between each vehicle being wide enough for each to turn about. A second rank would serve no useful purpose, whereas a second body of chariots some distance behind the first could have rendered invaluable support.

On the point of contact each charioteer would concentrate on steering his chariot towards an enemy vehicle opposite. Simultaneously, the chariot warrior would brace himself, levelling his thrusting spear for that eventual clash with his protagonist, now only metres away. As the lines inter-penetrated, the chariots would veer past each other, an unlucky warrior having been knocked from his vehicle by a well-aimed thrust. This action would be repeated all along the line.

After the opposing formations had passed through each other, surviving chariots would then attempt to turn about and engage in further combat. No doubt the mêlée would soon become confused, rapidly degenerating into individual duels. If either formation was backed up by a second wave of chariotry, or even infantry, their timely arrival could be decisive.

Rail-chariot

The rail-chariot appeared at the turn of the 13th century BC and soon replaced the box-chariot. From the various depictions of Mycenaean chariots on LH IIIB pottery, it seems that the new design consisted of little besides a platform and a grab-rail at waist-height or thereabouts, and stays by which the rail was held firm. The fundamental difference between the rail-chariot and its predecessor lies in the extreme lightness of the former, as revealed by the absence of breastwork or side panels.

Crew

It was common for one or both of the crew to carry round shields, while the chariot warrior alone was armed with a short spear. The sword was also shorter in length, the earlier rapier-type having been replaced by an efficient cut-and-thrust weapon with a broad, sometimes leaf-shaped blade (Naue II sword). Both crewmen wore a bronze or bronze-reinforced leather corselet that did not extend over the shoulders. Bronze greaves were worn either over fabric greaves or long woollen socks. A simple crested helmet completed the panoply, perhaps made from hardened leather reinforced with bronze strips or discs much like that worn by the foot-warriors on the B-side of the Warrior Vase (an artefact found in Mycenae, depicting the lives of the Mycenaean warriors).

Deployment

From what is known of chariot warfare it is unlikely that these second-stage vehicles were employed in battle en masse. On the contrary, it would seem probable that a chariot warrior, armed with a round shield and a short spear, would dismount to fight more readily than earlier Mycenaean chariotry, his charioteer retiring a short way from the drop-off point in order to await events. This tallies with the majority of the descriptions of chariot battles in the *Iliad*.

Scholars do concede that there is 'just the occasional hint of a realistic use of chariotry' (Greenhalgh 1973: 7), often referring to *Iliad* 4.293–309 when Nestor delivers a pre-battle harangue to the Pylian chariotry. He instructs the charioteers to control their teams so that they can charge in formation, the warriors to thrust with the spear from their chariot as 'the men before your time [*proteroi*] sacked tower and city' (*Iliad* 4.308). This passage, however, is simply dismissed by others as a historical archaism, Homer having some dim and distant recollection of what chariots had done in earlier times.

Homer portrays Nestor as nimble-witted and skilled in giving counsel (*Iliad* 1.248–522, 2.76–84, 7.324–344), having lived through two generations and now being king of Pylos in the third. Like all wise patriarchal figures, Nestor also enjoys reminiscing about his youth, a youth in which he had fought battles and gained experience of tactics that were now falling out of use.

The young Nestor had once led a successful cattle-raid deep into the territory of Elis, Pylos' northern neighbour. The 'bronze-armoured

Homeric chariot
In the *Iliad* chariots convey heroes to and from the battlefield, or from one part of the frontline to another, whereupon they dismount to duel. The charioteers, meanwhile, keep the vehicle at the ready to effect, if necessary, a rapid retreat or prompt pursuit (*Iliad* 2.464–466, 7.1–3, 8.58–59 [into battle]; 5.239–240, 11.527–530 [point-to-point]; 4.419–421, 6.103–105, 8.320–322, 11.47–49, 16.426–427 [dismount to fight]; 5.45–46, 8.157–158, 11.596–597 [retreat]; 8.191–197, 16.377–379, 20.498–501 [pursuit]). It is true that the chariot as a means of battlefield transport for a warrior was not its primary purpose in the chariot kingdoms of the Near East. However, once the box-chariot had fallen out of use and the rail-chariot had taken its place, the warrior-kings and chieftains of Mycenaean Greece used chariots to convey warriors to and from battle. To assume that the chariot is most effective tactically in the massed attack neglects the fundamental fact that there was no single legitimate tactical role for the war chariot.

It is the ancient writer Diodoros who notes that the tribes of Britain 'used chariots as tradition tells us the old Greek heroes did in the Trojan War' (5.21.5). True, Diodoros was on the lookout for Homeric parallels in Celtic society, and his account is somewhat anachronistic and based upon hearsay. Despite this, however, his statement can be expanded and elucidated upon by referring to the source from which it probably came, the *Commentaries* of C. Iulius Caesar. Caesar's description of British charioteers presents a marvellous picture of their skill and agility:

In chariot fighting the Britons begin by riding all over the field hurling javelins, and generally the terror inspired by the horses and the noise of the wheels are sufficient to throw their opponents' ranks into disorder. Then, after making their way between the cavalry squadrons, they jump down from their chariots and engage on foot. In the meantime their charioteers retire a short distance from the battle and place the chariots in such a position that their warriors, if hard pressed by numbers, have an easy means of retreat to their own lines. Thus they combine the mobility of cavalry with the staying power of infantry; and by daily training and practice they attain such proficiency that even on a steep incline they are able to control the horses at a full gallop, and to check and turn them in a moment. They can run along the chariot pole, stand on the yoke, and get back into the chariot as quick as lightning (Bellum Gallicum 4.33).

In Caesar's eyewitness account, only the running out along the draught pole is non-Homeric. Yet the Celtic chariot was open-fronted, thus enabling the chariot warrior to perform such acrobatic feats. The Homeric chariot, on the other hand, had a cab enclosed on three sides, made up of a steam-bent frame that probably stood at waist-height. *Iliad* 5.722–732 is the *locus classicus* for the construction of the Homeric chariot, with line 728 being of particular interest: 'with double chariot rails that circle about it'. Although this passage describes Hera's chariot, there are at least seven other references in the *Iliad* (5.262, 322, 10.475, 11.535, 16.406, 20.500–501, 21.38), which support the notion that the cab of a Homeric chariot was constructed in such a fashion.

Epeians' retaliate by investing the Pylian settlement of Thryoëssa. A relief force under Neleus, Nestor's father, marches post-haste to lift the siege, arriving outside Thryoëssa on the afternoon of the following day. Nestor, having been forbidden to ride into battle by his father because he 'was not yet skilled in the work of warfare' (*Iliad* 11.718), prepares to fight on foot. However, he manages to seize an enemy chariot, whereupon he joins the Pylian chariotry and charges the Epeians, overtaking 'fifty chariots, and for each of the chariots two men caught the dirt in their teeth beaten down under my spear' (*Iliad* 11.747–748).

There is no doubt that Nestor's instructions to his charioteers are a genuine look back to the days when Mycenaean chariots were deployed en masse for battle. For Nestor stresses that this was how 'the men before your time sacked tower and city' (*Iliad* 4.308), and this doctrine is qualified by his anecdote describing the chariot battle outside Thryoëssa. The Pylians charge the Epeians in formation, each warrior (plus young Nestor) fighting from the cab of his vehicle with a spear as Mycenaean warriors had done from their box-chariots.

Tactical changes

The rail-chariot and its crew were most certainly the product of a major change in Mycenaean chariot tactics, if not military organization in general. Witness the appearance of the Mycenaean horseman, as represented by LH IIIA-B terracotta figurines and pottery iconography, such as the LH IIIA krater decorated with a chariot preceded by a horseman. In all examples the horseman wears either a conical helmet or carries a short sword, or both. The eventual breakdown of the palace economies, and, therefore, the elaborate organization required to maintain chariot forces, may have hastened this development of horse-warriors.

The introduction of the rail-chariot may also be associated with the change in infantry equipment taking place at this time. The depictions of unarmoured foot-warriors on the Ship Fresco from Thera (LH IIA)

Three non-joining krater shards (LH IIIB) from Tiryns showing a rail-chariot, preceded by two foot-warriors carrying small, round shields and short spears. Note the hunting dog running alongside the chariot team. (National Archaeological Museum, Athens, 1511, 10548, 10549, photograph author's collection)

This painted relief from the mortuary temple of Hatshepsut, Deir el-Bahri depicts Egyptian 'strong arm boys' (*nakhtu-aa*), hand-to-hand fighters equipped with spear, battle-axe and shield. The officer in front also carries a cased composite bow. (Royal Museum, Edinburgh, photograph author's collection)

and the Lion Hunt dagger from Shaft Grave VI (LH I-IIB) indicate that the Mycenaeans had developed close-order formations equipped with thrusting spears and full-body shields. These were initially rectangular in shape, allowing them to meet edge-to-edge to form a continuous wall; they were hung from the shoulder, so the foot-warrior was able to wield his weapon in both hands. Archers and slingers could also operate from within the spear formation, no doubt deriving some protection from the shield wall. This 'tower shield' was possibly replaced, gradually, by the 'figure-of-eight' type, which had certain advantages over its predecessor. It was deeper, thereby increasing the shield's deflective qualities, while the 'waist' provided a gap to allow spears to protrude at hip-level from the shield wall. In contrast, the Warrior Vase depicts foot-warriors equipped with helmets, body armour and greaves, and carrying round shields (with central grip) and short spears. It appears that infantry tactics had developed from the rigid, densely packed shield wall formations into a more fluid style of fighting.

Three possible reasons exist for such a change during the twilight years of Mycenaean influence throughout the Aegean. First, the inability to train and organize long-spear formations. Second, long-spear formations were simply rendered obsolete by the needs of the time, such as the evolution of less formal battles once dominated by chariotry. Or, finally, the development of lighter and more flexible types of body armour suitable for foot-warriors that were by now fleet of foot and skilled with cut-and-thrust sword, short spear and round shield. In other words, foot-warriors suitably equipped for mobile combat often associated with raiding on land and at sea.

THE CHARIOT IN ACTION

According to a biblical prophecy, when this world ends the last cataclysmic battle will be fought at 'the place called in Hebrew, Armageddon' (Revelations 16:16). *Har megiddon*, 'the mountain of Megiddo', was also the site of the first chariot battle that can be reconstructed in some detail.

Megiddo

The strategic importance of the northern Syro-Palestinian city of Megiddo (Tell el-Mutesellim) lies in its location at the exit of Wadi 'Ara, the narrow defile that links the plain of Sharon, which extends along the seaboard between Joppa and Caesarea, with the plain of Jezreel (in Greek, Esdraelon). This was the line of the later Via Maris, the Roman highway that served as the arterial route between Egypt, Syria and Mesopotamia. Its commanding situation meant Megiddo was strongly fortified by Canaanites, Egyptians, and Israelites, and the Romans would later station a legion here, legio VI Ferrata. Whoever sat in Megiddo controlled this vital artery and consequently important areas of the Fertile Crescent.

In the spring of 1457 BC, with this fact clearly in mind, the king of Qadesh moved southward leading a coalition of Canaanite and Syrian princes. His main objective was to bar the northward advance of the pharaoh Thutmose III, who had decided to deal directly with the growing problems in Retennu that threatened the security of Egypt's north-eastern frontier.

Thutmose's response had been dynamic, for his army had only taken nine days to march from Egypt to Gaza, an average rate of 26km per day. From Gaza he advanced north to Yehem (El-Yâmôn) and here held a war council. The enemy was deployed within the immediate vicinity of Megiddo and the pharaoh had three possible routes along which he could approach their position. First, the direct route through the defile of Aruna (Wadi 'Ara), a pass of less than two chariots' width, which would allow him to appear from the hills about 2km from Megiddo. The second option was the northern route via the settlement of Djefty, which would position him west of Megiddo. Finally, the southern route leading to Taanach (Tell Ta'annak), some 8km south-east of Megiddo.

Thutmose's generals believed that the narrow, direct approach had to be avoided at all costs because it would be necessary for the Egyptians to move in line of column against a defending force deployed in line of

battle. The report of this war council as transmitted by the military scribe Tjaneni, along with all the textural evidence for Megiddo, is recorded in the Annals of Thutmose III, a hieroglyphic inscription in the temple of Amun-Ra at Karnak. At the council of war the generals asked the pharaoh:

> What is it like to go on this road, which becomes so narrow? It is reported that the foe is there, waiting on the outside, while they are becoming more numerous. Will not horse have to go after horse, and the army and the people similarly? Will the vanguard of us be fighting while the rearguard is waiting here in Aruna unable to fight? (Breasted 1927: 2.421)

The pharaoh, on the other hand, decided for reasons of prestige to choose the short and difficult route: 'They will say, these enemies whom Ra abominates: "Has his majesty set out on another road because he has become afraid of us?" – so they will speak' (Breasted 1927: 2.422).

Thutmose's decision, as it turned out, was a wise one, and may well have been based on his appreciation of intelligence reports. The Annals hint that the king of Qadesh expected the Egyptians to avoid the direct route for the same sound tactical reasons advanced by the Egyptian commanders in the war council. He had therefore despatched sizeable units to guard the other two approaches to Megiddo. It seems that military intelligence played a large part in formulating the battle plan, as the Annals suggest that spies informed Thutmose of the decision of the king of Qadesh to make a stand outside the city.

When the Egyptian vanguard debouched from the pass just after midday, the rearguard was still at Aruna, a six-hour march away. The generals now urged the pharaoh to halt the advance in order to permit the rear of the column to move up so that the entire army could engage the enemy:

> Let our victorious lord listen to us this time, and let our lord guard for us the rear of his army and his people. When the rear

of the army comes forth for us into the open, and then we shall fight against these foreigners, then we shall not trouble our hearts about the rear of the army. (Breasted 1927: 2.427)

Understanding the need to concentrate his forces, Thutmose bowed to the wisdom of his war council. A camp was therefore established south of Megiddo on the banks of the Qina stream, rations issued, and the footsore troops rested. That same evening, a royal proclamation declared: 'Prepare ye! Make your weapons ready, since one [the pharaoh] will engage in combat with that wretched enemy in the morning' (Breasted 1927: 2.429).

The 'wretched enemy' were still some distance away near Taanach to the south, and near the exit of the Djefty pass in the north. The king of Qadesh had been wrong-footed by the pharaoh's choice of route.

At sun-up Thutmose launched his attack. The army had been divided into three 'battles', one to attack the defenders in the north, another in the south, and the main 'battle', led personally by the pharaoh, was to strike at the enemy centre deployed outside Megiddo. The coalition forces were swept away in the ensuing engagement, the Egyptians pursuing them to the very walls of Megiddo, whose citizens had closed the gates thereby forcing the routers to 'Abandon their horses and their chariots of gold and silver, so that someone might draw them up into the town by hoisting on their garments' (Breasted 1927: 2.430).

Clearly, Thutmose could have pressed home his advantage and stormed Megiddo in its state of panic, but unfortunately his troops began to loot the enemy camp, taking not only plunder and prisoners but also the hands of the fallen as visible tokens of battle accomplishment. As Tjaneni (Thutmose's private secretary) bluntly put it: 'Now if only his majesty's army had not given up their hearts to capturing the possessions of the enemy, they would have captured Megiddo at this time' (Breasted 1927: 2.431).

Looting is an age-old pastime for the universal soldier, and a major concern for any commander wishing to maintain the objective once his forces have vanquished the opposition on the field of battle. At Megiddo the curse of looting meant that Thutmose had to settle for a formal siege. Since the city had an ample supply of water within its walls, it managed to hold out against the Egyptians for seven months.

The importance of its eventual capture is duly summed up in the proclamation the pharaoh delivered to his troops:

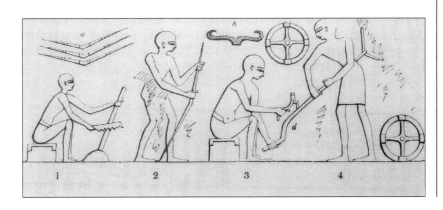

Pictorial representations verify that chariots were built in workshops employing woodworkers, metalworkers, and those skilled in leatherwork. (Reproduced from J. Gardner Wilkinson, *The Ancient Egyptians: Their Life and Customs*, John Murray, London, 1854)

Glue and rawhide were the usual binders in chariot construction, and here the currier finishes the body and framework of a chariot. (Reproduced from J. Gardner Wilkinson, *The Ancient Egyptians: Their Life and Customs*, John Murray, London, 1854)

Capture ye effectively, my victorious army! Behold all the foreign countries have been put in this town by command of Ra on this day; in as much as every prince of every northern country is shut up within it, for the capturing of Megiddo is the capturing of a thousand towns! (Breasted 1927: 2.432)

The most valuable booty of the victory probably came in the form of horses, of which the Egyptians captured 2,041 mares, 191 foals and six stallions. As the Egyptians were still importers of bloodstock, such numbers would have been an important addition to their chariot arm. Yet with the accent on mares, the pharaoh was obviously looking to establish studs in Egypt on a grand scale. Other spoils taken from the battlefield included 502 bows, 340 prisoners and 83 hands.

Also taken was the 'chariot wrought with gold' belonging to the king of Qadesh, the 'beautiful chariot, wrought with gold' belonging to the prince of Megiddo, and no less than 892 chariots of 'his wretched army' (Breasted 1927: 2.435). Two of the chariots from the tomb of Tutankhamun are conspicuous for their sumptuous hieroglyphic and relief decoration in gold and coloured inlay (Littauer and Crouwel 1985: 11–17, 19–23). It has been argued that chariots of wood overlaid with gold were normally reserved for parade, but according to the Annals, Thutmose himself fought at Megiddo in a chariot 'overlaid with electrum' (Breasted 2.430). There were 30 other chariots taken, thus making a grand total of 924 chariots. It seems there were at least a thousand chariots on the Canaanite side, and presumably the Egyptians brought a similar number.

CONCLUSION

Domestication of the horse took place on the Eurasian steppe, and if not here, then further west in the Ukraine, by peoples whose mobile economy was based on animal husbandry. While the horse lacked the stature and weight-carrying capacity required of it to endure the rigours of life as a true cavalry mount, a chariot team offered the swiftest means of travel, especially in the climatic conditions of the Near East. According to a Sumerian proverb, 'The horse, after he had thrown off his rider, said, "if my burden is always to be this, I shall become weak"' (Gordon 1958: 18).

Only when the horse grew larger under domestic care and selective breeding was there scope for cavalry. This was the military situation of the Assyrian kings, who deployed cavalry in addition to chariotry. Prior to this development, chariots remained the principal means of mobile warfare. Speaking of a tribe who live north of the Ister (Danube), Herodotos claims they have 'little, snub nosed, shaggy horses, with hair about four inches long all over their bodies. These horses cannot carry a man, but are very fast in harness, with the result that driving is here the rule' (5.9). Herodotos' observations on the equestrian habits of the Sigymae explain why earlier Bronze Age civilizations had yoked the horse to a chariot instead of riding it into battle.

BIBLIOGRAPHY

Anderson, J.K., 'Homeric, British and Cyrenaic chariots', *American Journal of Archaeology* 69, pp.349–52 (1965)

Azzaroli, A., *An Early History of Horsemanship*, E.J. Brill, Leiden (1985)

Beal, R.H., *The Organisation of the Hittite Military*, C. Winter, Heidelberg, (1992)

Breasted, J.H., *Ancient Records of Egypt*, vols. 2 and 3, University of Chicago Press, Chicago (1927)

Drews, R., *The End of the Bronze Age: Changes in Warfare and the Catastrophe ca. 1200 BC*, Princeton University Press, Princeton, (1993, 1995)

Faulkner, R.O., 'The battle of Megiddo', *Journal of Egyptian Archaeology* 28, pp.2–15 (1942)

Faulkner, R.O., 'Egyptian military organization', *Journal of Egyptian Archaeology* 39, pp.32–47 (1953)

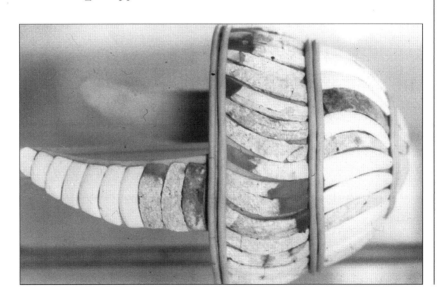

Boars' tusk helmet (LH IIIA) recovered from a warrior grave, North Cemetery at Knossos. When describing this type of helmet, Homer used such phrases as 'thongs of leather', 'felt', and 'the white teeth of a tusk-shining boar' (*Iliad* 10.261–265). (Author's collection)

Goedicke, H., *The Battle of Megiddo*, Halgo, Baltimore (2000)

Gordon, E.I., 'Sumerian animal proverbs and fables', *Journal of Cuneiform Studies* 12: pp.1–21, (1958)

Greenhalgh, P.A.L., *Early Greek Warfare*, Cambridge University Press, Cambridge (1973)

Greenhalgh, P.A.L., 'The Dendra charioteer', *Antiquity* 54, pp.201–5 (1980)

Healy, M., *New Kingdom Egypt*, Osprey (Elite 40), Oxford (1992, 2003)

Hyland, A., *Equus*, Batsford, London (1990)

Hyland, A., *The Horse in the Ancient World*, Sutton Publishing, Stroud (2003)

Littauer, M.A. and J.H. Crouwel, *Wheeled Vehicles and Ridden Animals in the Ancient Near East*, E.J. Brill, Leiden (1979)

Littauer, M.A. and J.H. Crouwel, 'Chariots in Late Bronze Age Greece', *Antiquity* 57, pp.187–92 (1983)

Littauer, M.A. and J.H. Crouwel, *Chariots and Related Equipment from the Tomb of Tut'ankhamun*, Griffith Institute, Oxford (1985)

Luckenbill, D.D., *Ancient Records of Assyria and Babylonia*, vols. 1 & 2, University of Chicago Press, Chicago (1926, 1927)

McDermott, B., *Warfare in Ancient Egypt*, Sutton Publishing, Stroud (2004)

McLeod, W.E., *Composite Bows from the Tomb of Tut'ankhamun*, Griffith Institute, Oxford (1970)

Moorey, P.R.S., 'The emergence of the light, horse-drawn chariot in the Near East', *World Archaeology* 18, pp.196–215 (1986)

Oppenheim, A.L., *Letters from Mesopotamia*, University of Chicago Press, Chicago (1967)

Partridge, R.B., *Fighting Pharaohs: Weapons and Warfare in Ancient Egypt*, Peartree, Manchester (2002)

Piggott, S., *The Earliest Wheeled Transport: from the Atlantic Coast to the Caspian Sea*, Thames & Hudson, London (1983)

Piggott, S., *Wagon, Chariot and Carriage: Symbol and Status in the History of Transport*, Thames & Hudson, London (1992)

Pritchard, J.B. (ed.), *Ancient Near Eastern Texts Relating to the Old Testament*, Princeton University Press, Princeton (1969)

Schulman, A.R., 'Egyptian representations of horsemen and riding in the New Kingdom', *Journal of Near Eastern Studies* 16, pp.263–71 (1957)

Schulman A.R., 'The Egyptian chariotry: a re-examination', *Journal of the American Research Centre in Egypt* 2, pp.75–98 (1963)

Schulman A.R., *Military Rank, Title and Organization in the Egyptian New Kingdom*, B. Hessling, Berlin (1964)

Shaw, I., *Egyptian Warfare and Weapons*, Shire Publishing, Princes Risborough (1991)

Snodgrass, A.M., 'The Linear B arms and armour tablets – again', *Kadmos* 4, pp.96–110 (1965)

Spalinger, A.J., *War in Ancient Egypt: the New Kingdom*, Blackwell, Oxford (2005)

Spruytte, J., *Early Harness Systems: Experimental Studies*, J.A. Allen, London (1983)

Stagakis, G., 'Homeric warfare practices', *Historia* 34, pp.127–52, (1985)

Stillman, N. and N. Tallis, *Armies of the Ancient Near East, 3000 BC to 539 BC*, Wargames Research Group, Worthing (1984)

Yadin, Y., *The Art of Warfare in Biblical Lands in the Light of Archaeological Discovery*, Weidenfeld & Nicholson, London (1963)

COLOUR PLATE COMMENTARY

A: SUMERIAN BATTLEWAGON
The Mesopotamian battlewagon was essentially worthless as a weapon of destruction. Yet, with all its shortcomings, it was a formidable instrument of intimidation. The psychological effect of a charging unit of battlewagons, especially against raw or unsteady troops, was sufficient to win it a staple place in the third millennium BC armies of Sumer.

Artistic representations of the battlewagon show a heavy vehicle with massive disc wheels and four long-eared equids hitched before it. The vehicle's carriage is narrow, wide enough for one occupant abreast, with a solid floor. The carriage front is high to offer protection to the charioteer, though the sides are low. The warrior standing on the rear platform steadies himself on the springless vehicle by holding the shoulders of the charioteer.

Though onagers and donkeys can run at speed, they make up for this with a foul temper, hence the basketwork muzzles on the headstalls. The method of harnessing is by simple rope collars; only the two central animals are yoked, with the two outriggers setting the pace for the whole team. The method of control, with reins and nose-rings, is for braking only. Frontal trappers, composed of leather strips, provide some protection to the team.

B: EGYPTIAN CHARIOT
In designing their chariots, the Egyptians deliberately sacrificed protection for the lightness so necessary to ensure speed. Made from light hardwoods, with an interwoven rawhide platform on which the two crewmen could comfortably stand abreast, an entire chariot weighed less than 30kg. This, combined with a sophisticated wheel construction, gave it a mobility that must have been very hard to match.

It was essential for an Egyptian warrior to acquire archery skills and to be capable of hitting a target from a speeding, lightweight chariot. Thus, considering the necessity of a close relationship between the warrior and his charioteer, the chariot crew would have honed their battle skills through regular practice together. One standard drill required an archer to fire from a fast-moving chariot at a series of standing targets. While the archer concentrated on shooting, his charioteer protected him with a shield and concentrated on driving the vehicle. The account of the archery skills of Amenhotep II indicates the chariot had to be driven at full gallop past a series of copper targets set on poles placed 12m apart. The warrior had to try to send a shaft clean through a target, or pierce it with more than one arrow.

C: HITTITE CHARIOT
Fighting from a chariot with a spear was possible, in spite of assertions to the contrary, and that is certainly how the Hittites used their three-man chariots. Michael Loades, a re-enactment specialist who tested the capabilities of a replica Hittite chariot, had no trouble in using a thrusting spear from the side of the vehicle at speed. Employing spear and chariot together was an innovation in weapons development. It represented new military tactics, originating in the Anatolia-Aegean area, based upon the chariot's aggressive use in close-quarter combat. The new weapons demanded different military skills and the employment of

Ivory inlay (LH IIIB) recovered from a chamber tomb, Spata, Attica. In the form of a warrior's head wearing a boars' tusk helmet, this once decorated a piece of wooden furniture. (National Archaeological Museum, Athens, 2055, photograph author's collection)

heavy body armour. It thus put new demands on the training of chariot warriors.

Specific drills would have been formulated so as to train the armoured spearmen to fight from within the chariot. In the heat of battle he would be expected to use his spear as an offensive weapon, which meant having the skill to single-handedly thrust it laterally so that he could strike down an enemy charioteer in a passing chariot. Regular training was essential, and one standard drill required warriors to thrust their spear from a moving chariot at a series of targets represented by straw-filled dummies suspended from wooden supports.

D: MYCENAEAN BOX-CHARIOT

Ownership of a chariot was an expensive and time-consuming business. Horses suited for teamwork had to be selected, trained and exercised regularly, fed and watered. The chariot itself required a great deal of care, since the component parts consisted almost exclusively of organic materials, which were subject to extreme wear and tear. While the large-scale use of chariots was possible for the chariot kingdoms of the Near East, such sophisticated, high-status vehicles were deployed only to a limited extent in mainland Greece. The Linear B tablets reveal to us the immense resources required by Mycenaean warrior-kings to maintain even a small chariot arm. Yet it was still an instrument of war and a key resource of the palace army.

A chariot warrior equipped with the Dendra panoply mounts his vehicle, the robust box-chariot, while the charioteer steadies the chariot team. Apart from the encumbrance factor, this armour was effective. Its curved surfaces would have helped to deflect glancing blows and, although a direct thrust from a pointed weapon would have punctured the bronze, a padded undergarment would have helped to absorb any attack. The front of the protective skirt is tied loosely to allow the warrior to mount the vehicle.

See plate for full details.

A rail-chariot containing two crewmen on a krater shard (LH IIIB) from the 'granary', Mycenae. One warrior is armed with a spear, but both are carrying small, round shields. (Archaeological Museum, Nauplion, 8357, photograph author's collection)

E: MYCENAEAN RAIL-CHARIOT

The bronze-clad heroes of the *Iliad* rode into battle in their chariot, but left their horses in the care of the charioteer just outside missile range while they themselves dismounted to fight on foot. Despite Homer's clear-cut picture of chariots in combat, and the known parallels in other 'heroic' societies, most scholars dismiss this as nonsense. They believe that chariots ought to have been used quite differently in battle, either carrying archers and serving as firing-platforms, or carrying heavily armed warriors with thrusting spears and serving as fighting-platforms. Yet considerations other than pure military efficiency always play a part in determining the ways of war in any society.

In the late Mycenaean period chariot design altered and a less robust vehicle appeared. The rail-chariot is probably the best candidate for the 'Homeric chariot', and its introduction can be linked with significant changes in chariot tactics. This reconstruction uses iconographic detail from 'chariot kraters', which show chariots simply consisting of a platform and a grab-rail. The chariot warriors wear metallic or composite body armour, including helmets and greaves, and carry small shields. Most fighting was now done on foot with the spear used in combat, supported by a very strong cut-and-thrust sword.

F: BATTLE OF MEGIDDO, 1457 BC

The two forces at Megiddo both use chariots as fast-moving archery platforms, hence the need for plenty of space between vehicles with one battle line supported by another set some way behind. Here we see Thutmose's chariot 'battle' advancing at a canter towards that of the king of Qadesh,

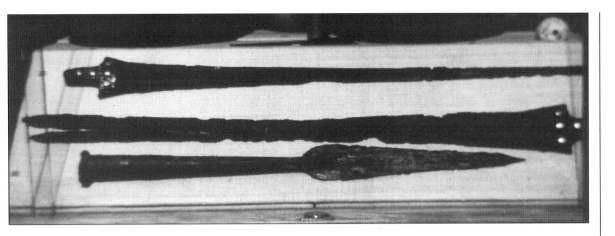

which forms the Canaanite centre. The king is busy ordering his squadrons in preparation to counter-charge the Egyptians.

In theory, the opposing lines of advancing chariots would have slipped around or through each other, the archers continuing their firing by facing the rear of their vehicles and letting off one or two shots at their opponents as they receded. Then the two forces, if they were still cohesive, would have wheeled around and begun their second charge, this time from the opposite direction. Yet so swift and decisive was Thutmose's chariot-led charge that the defeated Canaanites barely managed to escape into Megiddo. In their haste to take shelter within the walled city, the fleeing troops were said to have inadvertently locked out the king of Qadesh and the prince of Megiddo, who had to be dragged unceremoniously on to the battlements by their clothing.

G: CHARIOT CLASH AT QADESH, 1274 BC

Qadesh remains a popular chariot battle with military historians because of the detailed pictorial representations left by Rameses II on the walls of temples at Thebes, Karnak, Luxor, Abydos and Abu Simbel. A hieroglyphic inscription, which describes each battle scene as it unfolds before the viewer, accompanies these images. To the Egyptian version of Qadesh may be added that contained in a badly damaged treaty letter written in Akkadian long after the event by Rameses II to Hattusilis III, who had usurped his brother Muwatallis II.

As Rameses' second army, that of Ra, marched up from the south Muwatallis II, the Hittite king, launched his attack by despatching 2,500 chariots in four bodies across the Orontes via a ford just below the fortified city of Qadesh. The Egyptian record describes how these chariots 'came forth from the southern side of Qadesh, and they cut through the army of Ra in its middle, while they were marching without knowing and without being drawn up for battle' (Breasted 1927: 3.311). The army of Ra broke in panic and fled up against the army of Amun to the north, which as a result also fell into confusion and incipient flight. The Hittites followed up in hot pursuit and finally encircled the Egyptian camp. Though Rameses was 'beloved of Amun-Ra, great in victories', his engagement with the Hittites at Qadesh was a near disaster caused by an elementary failure of military intelligence. Nevertheless, Rameses' personal leadership and tactical dexterity in the swirling chariot battle saved him at the decisive moment. Like Napoleon at Marengo, he was to snatch victory from the jaws of defeat.

ABOVE **Spearhead (LH I-IIB) from Shaft Grave IV, Grave Circle A, Mycenae. Remarkable for its size, it was undoubtedly attached to the thrusting spear wielded by a chariot warrior. (National Archaeological Museum, Athens, 446, photograph author's collection)**

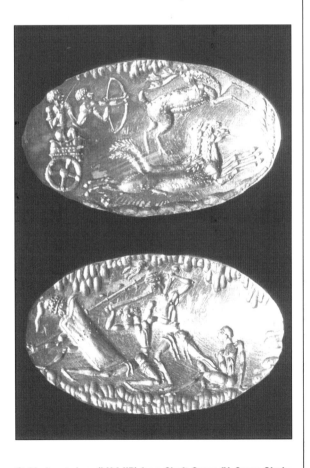

Gold signet rings (LH I-IIB) from Shaft Grave IV, Grave Circle A, Mycenae. The upper ring is engraved with a scene illustrating a bow-armed warrior hunting from his box-chariot. (National Archaeological Museum, Athens, photograph author's collection)

INDEX